PIANO
VOCAL
GUITAR

CHART HITS OF 2011 2012

ISBN 978-1-4584-2299-6

HAL•LEONARD®
CORPORATION
7777 W. BLUEMOUND RD. P.O. BOX 13819 MILWAUKEE, WI 53213

Visit Hal Leonard Online at
www.halleonard.com

THE ADVENTURES OF RAIN DANCE MAGGIE

Words and Music by ANTHONY KIEDIS,
FLEA, CHAD SMITH
and JOSH KLINGHOFFER

Lip - stick junk - ie, de - bunk ___ the all in one, she came back wear - ing a smile. ___

___ Look - in' like some - one drugged me; they want -

CODA

Instrumental solo

Solo ends You've got the wrong _____ girl, _____ but not for

long, _____ girl. _____ It's in the song, _____ girl, _

BRIGHTER THAN THE SUN

Words and Music by COLBIE CAILLAT
and RYAN TEDDER

Moderately

Stopped _ me on the cor - ner. Swear _ you hit _ me like a vi - sion I, I, I was - n't ex - pect - ing, but who _ am I _____ to tell _ fate where it's s'pposed _ to go

Read it; it's signed __ and de-liv-ered. Let's seal it 'cause we go to-geth-er like

D.S. al Coda I

pea-nuts and Pay-Days, Mar-ley and reg-gae, and ev-'ry-bod-y needs to get a chance __ to say... __

Coda I

Ev-'ry-thing is like a white-out __

__ 'cause we shick-a, shick-a shine down, __ e-ven when the, when the light's out, __

CRAWLING BACK TO YOU

Words and Music by CHRIS DAUGHTRY
and MARTI FREDERIKSEN

Slowly

Les - sons __ learned, __ with bridg - es __ burned to __ the ground;

__ and it's too late __ now to put out the fire. __

Ta - bles __ turned, __ and I'm the one __ who's burn - ing __ now. __ Well, I'm

JUST A KISS

Words and Music by HILLARY SCOTT,
DALLAS DAVIDSON, CHARLES KELLEY
and DAVE HAYWOOD

Female:
Ly - in' here _ with you _ so close to me, ___ it's hard to fight _ these feel-

- in's when it feels _ so hard to breathe. _ I'm caught up in __ this mo-

* *Recorded a half step lower.*

HEARTBEAT

Words and Music by JOSEPH KING
and ISAAC SLADE

heart - beat. _ And, oh, _____ you're com - in' a - round, _

_____ com - in' a - round, com - in' a - round. _ If you can love some-bod - y, love _ 'em all the same. You got - ta
(D.S.) *Vocal ad lib.*

love some-bod - y, love _ 'em all the same. I'm sing - in', oh, _____ I'm feel - in' your _
(D.S.) *ad lib. ends*

To Coda ⊕

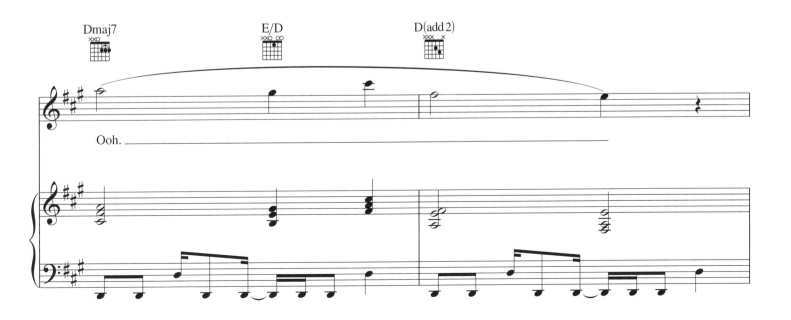

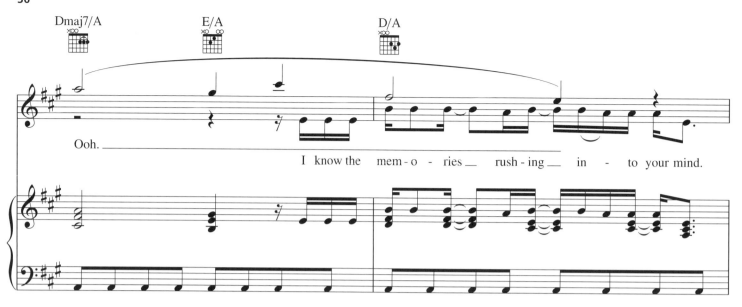

IT WILL RAIN

from the Summit Entertainment film
THE TWILIGHT SAGA: BREAKING DAWN – PART 1

Words and Music by BRUNO MARS,
PHILIP LAWRENCE and ARI LEVINE

Moderate groove

If you ev - er leave _ me, ba - by,

leave some mor - phine at ___ my door. ___

'Cause it would take a whole lot of med - i - ca - tion _____

MR. KNOW IT ALL

Words and Music by ESTHER DEAN,
BRIAN SEALS, BRETT JAMES
and DANTE JONES

MOVES LIKE JAGGER

Words and Music by ADAM LEVINE,
BENJAMIN LEVIN, AMMAR MALIK
and JOHAN SCHUSTER

With energy and a groove

Oh, _____ now.

Oh.

Just shoot for the stars _

-ed. I put on a show, ___ now we're nak - ed. You say I'm a kid, ___
___ it wher - ev - er you want, ___ get in - side ___ it. And you wan - na steer, ___

Em7

___ my e - go is big. ___ I don't give a sh**. ___
___ but I'm shift - in' gear. ___ I'll take it from here. ___

Bm7

And it goes __ like this: ___ Take me by the tongue and I'll know _ you.

Em7

Kiss me 'til you're drunk and I'll show _ you all the moves like Jag - ger. I've got the

NEVER SAY NEVER

from THE KARATE KID

Words and Music by JUSTIN BIEBER,
NASRI ATWEH, THADDIS HARRELL, OMARR RAMBERT,
ADAM MESSINGER and JADEN SMITH

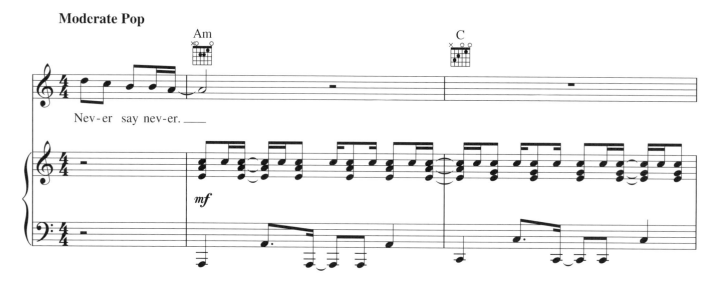

Moderate Pop

Nev-er say nev-er. ____

See, I

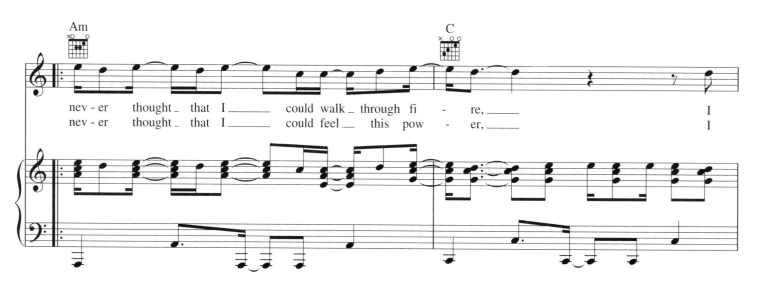

nev-er thought ___ that I _____ could walk ___ through fi - re, _____ I

nev-er thought ___ that I _____ could feel ___ this pow - er, _____ I

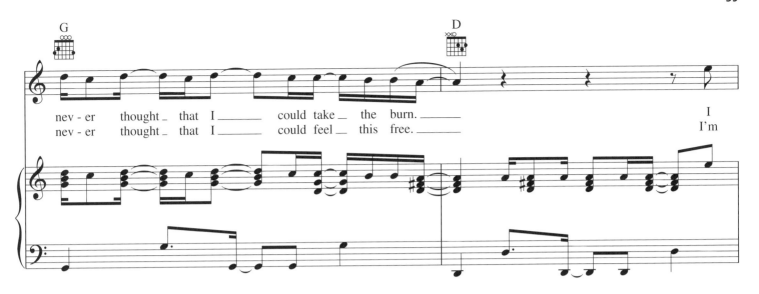

G   D

nev - er thought _ that I _____ could take _ the burn. _____

nev - er thought _ that I _____ could feel _ this free. _____

I

I'm

Am   C

nev - er had ___ the strength _ to take _ it high - er _____

strong e - nough _ to climb ___ the high - est tow - er _____

un -

and I'm

G   D

til I reached _ the point ___ of no _ re - turn. _____

fast e - nough _ to run ___ a - cross _ the sea. _____

And there's

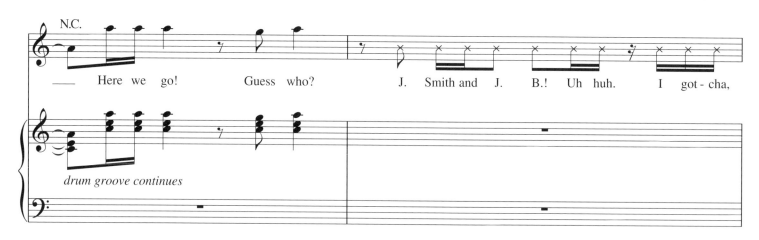

N.C.

_____ Here we go! Guess who? J. Smith and J. B.! Uh huh. I got - cha,

drum groove continues

lit - tle bro. I can han - dle him. Hold up, _____ a'right? I can han - dle him. Now

he's big - ger than me, _____ tall - er than me, and he's old - er than me _____ and strong - er than me. And

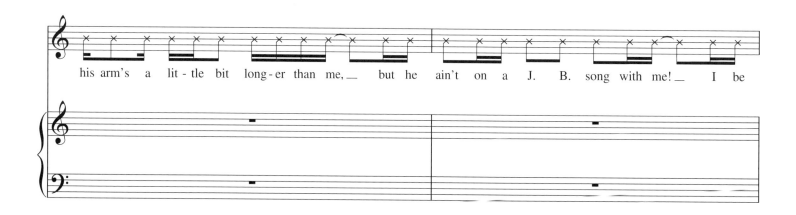

his arm's a lit - tle bit long - er than me, _____ but he ain't on a J. B. song with me! _____ I be

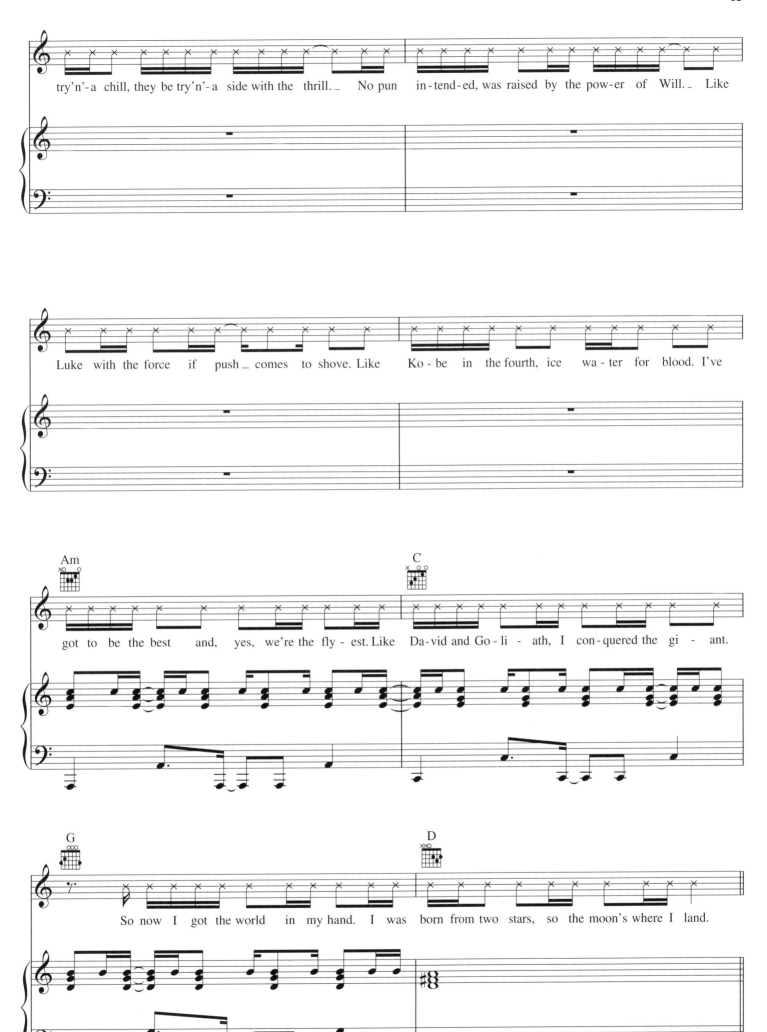

NOTHING

Words and Music by DANIEL O'DONOGHUE,
MARK SHEEHAN, STEPHEN KIPNER
and ANDREW FRAMPTON

PARADISE

Words and Music by GUY BERRYMAN,
JON BUCKLAND, WILL CHAMPION,
CHRIS MARTIN and BRIAN ENO

SHAKE IT OUT

Words and Music by FLORENCE WELCH,
THOMAS HULL and PAUL EPWORTH

Re - grets col - lect_____ like old friends, here to re - live_____

_____ your dark - est mo - ments. I can see no way, I can see no way._____

And all of the ghouls_____ come out to play. And ev - er - y de - mon wants his pound of

SOMEONE LIKE YOU

Words and Music by ADELE ADKINS
and DAN WILSON

YOÜ AND I

Words and Music by
STEFANI GERMANOTTA

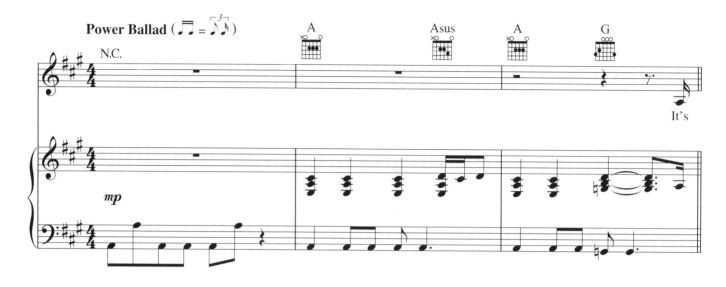

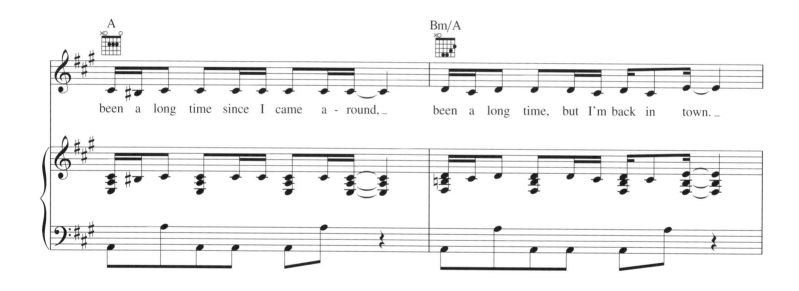

been_ two years since I let you_ go._ I could-n't lis-ten to a joke or_ rock and roll.__

Mus-cle cars_ drove a truck right through my heart._ On my

birth-day you sang me _"Heart of_ Gold"_ with a gui-tar_ hum-min' and_ no clothes._

D.S. al Coda

This time I'm not leav-in' with-out you._ Oh,_____ oh,_____

I. _____ You __ and I. __ I. _____ It's

been a long time __ since I came a - round, __ been a long time, __ but I'm back in town. __ And

this time I'm not leav - in' with - out you. ____

TONIGHT TONIGHT

Words and Music by EVAN BOGART,
LINDY ROBBINS, NASH OVERSTREET,
EMANUEL KIRIAKOU and RYAN FOLLESEE

Moderate Pop Rock

U - no, dos, tres. It's been a real-ly, real-ly messed - up week:
woke up with a strange tat - too.

sev-en days of tor - ture, sev-en days of bit-ter, and my girl-friend went and cheat-ed on me.___ She's a
Not sure how I got it, not a dol-lar in my pock - et. And it kind - a looks___ just___ like___ you,

Cal - i - for - nia dime,___ but it's time for me to quit her. La, la, la, what-ev - er.
mixed with Zach___ Ga - li - fia - na - kis. Uh.___